Marvelous Month-by-Month

Writing Prompts

250 Knock-Their-Socks-Off Writing Prompts to Inspire Super Writing All Year Long!

By Justin McCory Martin

S C H O L A S T I C
PROFESSIONAL BOOKS

New York • Toronto • London • Auckland • Sydney
Mexico City • New Delhi • Hong Kong • Buenos Aires

Dedication

To Diane Caldwell—a wonderful aunt and inspiring teacher

Cover design by Norma Ortiz
Cover artwork by Amy Vangsgard
Interior design by Sydney Wright
Interior artwork by Brian Floca

ISBN: 0-439-22250-8
Copyright © 2001 by Justin McCory Martin
All rights reserved.
Printed in the U.S.A.

Contents

Introduction 4

Writing Prompts

September 5

October 11

November 17

December 23

January 29

February 35

March 41

April 47

May 53

June 59

Introduction

Writing can be a deeply satisfying activity for kids. It's a great outlet for their creativity, one that lends itself to wild flights of fancy. It's also a wonderful vehicle for personal expression, more so now than ever in this age of e-mail.

But writing is also tough. Simply staring at a blank piece of paper is no way to get started. It's just too discouraging, when what is needed is encouragement and plenty of it. If only kids can start with the seed of an idea, their imaginations can flower. Writing can become an activity that's both exciting and enriching.

That's the purpose of the prompts contained in this book. Think of them as a little push to help your students get started, the same kind of push that any writer—even the most gifted veteran—naturally needs.

The prompts are organized by the ten months of the school year. Most of them are tied to specific events in a given month. For example, October includes a selection of Halloween-related prompts and June is full of those with summer themes. There are also prompts pegged to the anniversaries of historic happenings, like the Wright Brothers' famous flight (December 17); prompts tied to the birthdays of famous children's authors such as Theodor Geisel (March 2); and even some that relate to unusual dates such as Elephant Appreciation Day (September 22).

Kids will find that the prompts send them off in all kinds of directions, urging them to write stories, poems, songs, and mini-essays. The emphasis is on variety—interesting exercises spur interesting writing. Kids are even encouraged to write rap songs, e-mails, petitions, sports stories, and gossip columns—all in an effort to get those creative juices flowing.

September

① Back-to-School List

It's the beginning of a new school year. Make a list of the top ten most important things you will need for school. This will help you get started: You'll need your own desk, some paper, some pencils. What else? Think of at least ten other items.

② The Rap on Summer

This past summer, did you have fun in the sun? Did you swim with your friend Tim? Write a rap song that describes what you did this summer. Rap about all your good times and make sure it rhymes.

③ New School-Year's Resolutions

In January, people often make New Year's resolutions. They promise themselves that during the coming year they will change their lives in good ways. September is the beginning of the school year. Maybe there are some things you would like to do differently this school year. Maybe you want to improve at math or learn how to play soccer. Write down five New School-Year's Resolutions.

Dear Diary

Start a back-to-school diary. What subjects are you studying? What are some fun activities that you have done? Have you made any new friends? Each day during the first week of school write down your thoughts.

Photographic Memory

Look at a photograph in a magazine or newspaper for one minute. Study it very carefully. Then, put the photograph away where you can't see it. Write down every single detail that you can remember.

Bothered in Boston

September is Children's Good Manners Month. Pretend you write an advice column in the newspaper called "Ask the Manners Expert." Here's a letter you receive: "Dear Manners Expert, I like my friend Josh. But when we eat lunch in the cafeteria he always talks with his mouth full. How can I make him stop this without hurting his feelings? Signed, Bothered in Boston." Now, write an answer and give some good advice on good manners. Start out, "Dear Bothered in Boston, . . ."

Grabmunch for Thought

Here are some made-up names for very common things. Sun = Brighto. House = Livebox. Car = Gobox. Person = Smartbot. Food = Grabmunch. Talk = Yakyak. Write a story using all of these made-up words. This will help you get started: "Two smartbots were driving in a gobox. They were yakyaking about . . ."

In Reverse

Tell the story of coming to school this morning, backwards. This will be tough. Waking up was the first thing you did. But in a backwards tale, it becomes the end of your story. Here's the beginning of your story: "I arrived at school."

3001: A Space Oddity

The popular show *Star Trek* was first shown on TV on September 8, 1966. *Star Trek* is an example of what's known as *science fiction*. It's a type of story about the future that's full of exciting inventions like time-travel machines. What do you think the future will be like? Write your own science fiction story full of rocket rides, space aliens, and cool gadgets.

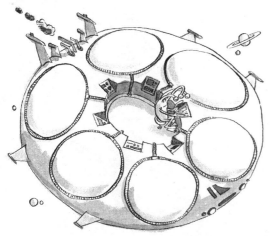

Festival of the Prunes

Each year on September 9 and 10, Yuba City, California, holds a Prune Festival. That sounds pretty silly, right? What do you think happens at the Prune Festival? Is there a prune toss? Do they crown a really wrinkly person as Mr. or Miss Prune? Write a story about what you think happens at the Yuba City Prune Festival.

Summer.com

It's a new school year. But what did you do this past summer? Create your own pretend Summer.com web site so you can remember all the fun you had. Did you go on vacation? Did you have some favorite summer songs? What flavors of ice cream did you eat? Make lists, draw pictures, and write short stories for your very own Summer.com site.

Town Anthem

On September 13, 1814, Francis Scott Key wrote the "Star Spangled Banner," our country's national anthem. Make up the words of an anthem for your town. You can mention local sports teams or foods that your town is famous for.

The Riddler

Do you like riddles? Here's one: *What has teeth, but cannot eat?* Answer: *A comb.* Come up with some riddles of your own. Write them on one side of a piece of paper; write answers on the other. When you're done, share them with a classmate.

Big Whopper

A really ridiculous story that isn't true is called a *whopper*. Each year on September 16, the town of New Harmony, Indiana, holds a "Big Whopper" contest. Dream up the biggest whopper you can and write it down.

Class Constitution

On September 17, 1787, the leaders of the United States agreed on the Constitution. The Constitution is a very important document. It spells out many of the rules for making the United States a good place to live. Create your own School Constitution, with rules such as "use quiet voices in the classroom" and "walk in the hallways."

Clowning Around

Clowns from all over the United States attend Clownfest. It's held in Seaside Heights, New Jersey. It starts each year on September 17 and runs for five days. Make up a clown of your own and give him or her a name. Then, write a story describing the adventures and misadventures of your clown.

Trading Cards

Use two index cards for this exercise. Label one "Character" and the other "Place." On the Character Card, write down a type of character. It can be anything: a genie, a farmer, a world-champion ping-pong player. On the Place Card, list a location. Again, it can be anywhere: Kansas, Mars, a shopping mall. Trade your Character Card with one classmate and your Place Card with another. Write a story featuring the character and place you wind up with.

Mini-Dictionary

Samuel Johnson was born on September 18, 1709. He created the very first English language dictionary. Here are ten words: *sausage, tennis, school, rain, gorilla, wristwatch, rocket, peach, movie, computer*. Think of good definitions for these words and create your own mini-dictionary. Because this is a dictionary, remember to put your words in alphabetical order.

Elephant Appreciation Day

September 22 is officially Elephant Appreciation Day. Go to the library or get on the Internet and do some research about these fascinating animals. Then, write down ten facts about elephants.

All About Neptune

On September 23, 1846, the planet Neptune was discovered by astronomers. Do some research to learn about this planet. How large is Neptune and how far is it from Earth? Write a mini-report about Neptune that includes your own ideas about what might be discovered in the future if a spaceship lands on the planet.

Snail Mail

There's regular mail that arrives in the mailbox. And there's e-mail that shows up on your computer. Imagine another kind of mail: catmail or watchmail or superball mail. Write a message to a friend using your strange new kind of mail.

Wild Fans

What is your favorite sport—basketball, football, gymnastics? And who is your favorite athlete? Pretend you are a reporter for a TV show called "Wild Fans." What questions would you want to ask your favorite athlete? Make up the answers that he or she would give to your questions.

Whale of a Tale

Shamu the orca whale was born on September 26, 1985. Shamu was the first orca born in captivity that survived and grew to be an adult. Do some research on orcas. Then, imagine that you are a trainer for an orca. What will you name it? What tricks will you teach it? Write a whale of a tale about your adventures.

Add Those Adjectives

"The man put on his coat and walked down the street to his car." This is a pretty boring sentence, right? But add some adjectives to make it more interesting, like this: "The angry man put on his heavy coat and walked down the dark street to his fancy car." Rewrite the sentence three times using various colorful adjectives.

Imperfect Ira Saves the World!

The fourth week of September is National Imperfection Week. Pretend that the mascot for this week is a boy named Imperfect Ira. Imperfect Ira brushes his hair with a toothbrush, always forgets to tie his shoes, and his favorite sandwich is a slice of bread between two pieces of bologna. But guess what! Imperfect Ira has to save the world from an invasion of three-legged monsters. Write a story and describe how Imperfect Ira saves the day.

October

Remember September

Now it's October. September was last month. Try to remember all the things that happened to you in September. Make a list of ten memories from last month.

We Are Family

Autumn seems like a good time to create a family tree. List as many relatives as you can think of: brothers and sisters, aunts and uncles. Go back as far as you can to your grandparents or even your great-grandparents. Write down descriptions of the various people in your family tree.

A Fable

A *fable* is a story that teaches an important lesson. Aesop was famous for his fables such as the "The Tortoise and the Hare." In this story, the Tortoise and the Hare race. The Hare is so sure he will beat the slow Tortoise that he doesn't try very hard. To his surprise, the Tortoise actually wins the race. The lesson of the fable: Always try hard or you might be surprised. Write your own fable, and be sure to include a helpful lesson at the end.

29

School Lunch Menu

October 8 through October 14 is National School Lunch Week. Create a menu of different foods that you would like to have each day of this special week. Remember, don't just pick your favorite foods. Your choices should be nutritious, too.

30

What's Irking Gilbert Grouch?

October 15 is National Grouch Day. Write a story about a character named Gilbert Grouch. This will get you started: "Gilbert Grouch woke up on the wrong side of the bed once again. He fixed his usual breakfast, bacon and eggs. As usual, he thought it tasted awful. Then, he put on his least favorite shirt and . . ."

31

Breezy Tale

Autumn is here and leaves are falling. Tell a story from the point of view of a single leaf. Give your leaf a name. Think about what kind of tree it lives in. Describe its trip down, down to the ground. Then what happens?

32

Time Capsule

On a piece of paper, write down some important facts about the present time in history. Who is the U.S. president? What are some popular TV shows or movies or songs? Place the paper inside an envelope. Label the envelope "Time Capsule" and seal it. You can hold on to this envelope as long as you like. If you open it in one year, or five years, or even twenty years, you'll have a reminder of what things used to be like.

Nickname Game

The musician John Birks Gillespie was born on October 21, 1917. Everyone called him "Dizzy" Gillespie. That was his *nickname*. Do you have a nickname? If so, why were you given this nickname? If not, think of a nickname for yourself and explain why you chose it.

Monster Diary

Create an imaginary Monster Diary for the days leading up to Halloween on October 31. Here's a sample entry to help you get started: "October 22. Today on the way to school I noticed that the bus was being driven by a ghost. I screamed very loudly." Now, write your own hair-raising diary, and include all the monsters, ghouls, and goblins you can think of.

Count On It!

Finish the following story. Make it go all the way up to ten. "One day, two sisters named Jill and Jenna ran into three . . ."

Just the Opposite

Salt and *pepper* are opposites. So are *up* and *down*. Pick out a passage in a favorite book or newspaper article. Now, rewrite it using opposites whenever you can. For example, the "short man" becomes the "tall woman."

Rainforest Petition

World Rainforest Week is October 21 through October 29. Do some research on rainforests. Then, write a *petition* to save the rainforest. A petition is a special letter that asks people to take a particular action. Make sure to give reasons why it's important to save the rainforest. This will help you get started on your petition. "I, (your name here), want to ask the citizens of the world to help save the rainforest. Rainforests are important because—"

(38) Weird Jennifer Anderson

October 23 is the birthday of singer and comedian "Weird Al" Yankovic. He changes the words of famous songs around to create his own silly versions. One of his most popular songs is "Eat It" instead of "Beat It," the hit song by Michael Jackson. First, place a "Weird" in front of your own name. Next, write a silly version of a favorite song.

(39) Abbreviation Creation

U.S. stands for "United States." S.O.S. stands for "Save Our Ship." These are called *abbreviations*. Create five abbreviations of your own, such as I.C.W.F.R., which stands for "I Can't Wait For Recess!"

(40) A to Z Tale

It's October 26. To celebrate, write a story in which you use all 26 letters of the alphabet, *A* to *Z*. Some letters are really tough, such as *Q* and *X* and *Z*. But here's a tip: You can use a letter in the middle or at the end of a word. For example, the word *box* uses the letter *X*.

(41) Synonym Speedway

A *synonym* is a word that has the same meaning as another word. Spend one minute writing down as many synonyms for the word "big" as you can think of. Hint: There are a huge number of synonyms for "big." Now, on your mark, get set, go!

(42) Halloween Carols

During December, people often sing Christmas carols. You may know some popular carols such as "Silent Night" and "Deck the Halls." But no one ever sings Halloween carols. Wouldn't it be cool if the holiday had its own special songs such as "Scary Night" or "Spook the Halls"? Make up a Halloween carol that's fun to sing and will frighten listeners so their hair stands on end.

Pumpkin Power

Halloween has plenty of monsters. But it needs a good superhero. Write a short script for a movie about Jill-O'-Lantern, crime-fighting pumpkin and monster avenger.

Spork It Over

Sometimes when you eat at a fast-food restaurant, they will have a special utensil called a *spork*. It's a combination of a spoon and a fork. What would you call a combination of a bicycle and a car, then? A bicycar, maybe? Think up five new combo words of your own. Make sure you write down their definitions, too.

Interview with the Purple-Crested Fiend

Imagine there's a monster called the Purple-Crested Fiend. It sounds pretty scary, right? But you must have lots of questions. What does it look like? What does it eat? Think of ten questions for the Purple-Crested Fiend. Then, exchange your questions with a class-mate. Answer your classmate's ten questions. Your classmate will answer your ten questions. Then everyone will know everything about the Purple-Crested Fiend.

Gold Medal, A-1, Grand-Prizewinning Invention

What do you think is the most important invention ever? Do you think it's fire, or the wheel, or maybe the computer? Write about the invention that you think is most important in the whole history of the world.

Cool Costume

What would you like to be for Halloween? Would you like to be a pirate, a tiger, or maybe a rock star? Describe the coolest costume that you can possibly imagine.

Crosswords

It is possible to cross the words "Texas" and "melt." Both include the letter "e." That's where you cross them. On a piece of paper, cross as many words as you possibly can. Remember, it's possible to cross a word more than once. For example, you can cross the word "example" with words such as "pet," "map," and "pillow."

Going Batty

Unlike many favorite Halloween ghouls and goblins, bats are real animals. They are very interesting, too. Did you know, for example, that they are not birds? They are mammals just like humans. You can learn more about bats from books or by looking in the encyclopedia or on the Internet. Do some research and write a mini-report full of true facts about these fascinating animals.

One More for Rushmore

Mount Rushmore was completed on October 31, 1941. It's a monument in South Dakota that features the faces of four American presidents carved into a mountainside. The presidents are George Washington, Thomas Jefferson, Abraham Lincoln, and Theodore Roosevelt. What if you could add another face to Mount Rushmore? Who would you choose? It doesn't have to be another president. It can be anyone you consider a hero. Write about the new person that you would add to Mount Rushmore.

November

Author, Author

November 1 is National Author's Day. In honor of this day, try your hand at being an author. Finish the following story: "This was truly amazing. Darrell and Katie could not believe it. If you opened the special door, on the other side was . . ."

Fearless Fiona and the Temple of the Amazon

King Tut's tomb was discovered in Egypt on November 4, 1922. Imagine that you made an exciting archaeological find: the Temple of the Amazon, maybe, or the Lost City of Antarctica. Give yourself a cool explorer's name like Fearless Fiona and write about your discovery in an Adventure Log.

Multiple Mel

Multiple Mel can do the following things:
A) Say something funny
B) Do a somersault
C) Eat something
D) Go someplace different
E) Say, "Awesome!"

Pick out ten letters among *A* through *E* in any order. For example, you could choose CECADDBCAE. That means Multiple Mel eats something (letter *C*), then says "Awesome!"(letter *E*), then eats something else (letter *C*), and so on. That might lead to the following Multiple Mel adventure: "Multiple Mel ate a cantaloupe and shouted out, 'Awesome!' and then . . ." Pick your ten letters first. Then, write your own Multiple Mel adventure.

Yard Skiing

James Naismith was born on November 6, 1861. He invented the game of basketball. Can you name a sport you would like to invent? Write down the rules and describe how it is played.

Coining a Coin

There's a new one-dollar coin featuring the Native American hero Sakajawea. Pretend you are creating your own new coin. How much would it be worth? What famous person would you feature on it and why?

Huge Tale

A Tall Tale is a story that is simply too strange to be believed. Here's an example: Once, a boy blew a bubblegum bubble the size of a hot-air balloon. He floated up into the air and traveled all the way to China. Make up your own Tall Tale. Really stretch your mind so that yours will actually be a Huge Tale.

X-Ray Vision

The X-ray was discovered on November 8, 1895. An X-ray makes it possible to see inside of things. Imagine that you have your own X-ray machine. What if you went home and found three boxes in your room: one huge, one medium-sized, and one tiny. You could use the X-ray to see inside the boxes, right? Use your imagination and describe what you see inside the three boxes.

58

Kid TV

The show *Sesame Street* first appeared on television on November 10, 1969. It had popular characters such as Kermit the Frog and the Cookie Monster. If you could create a children's show, what would you name it? Who would be some of the characters? Now, write a short script of your very own kids' TV show.

59

Don't Trash It!

November 12 is America Recycles Day. Maybe you already recycle cans and newspapers in your home. Make a list of ten other things people can do to help the environment.

60

Book Report

National Children's Book Week is November 13 through 19. What is your favorite book? Write a book report in which you discuss the characters and the story and explain why you especially like this book.

61

Strange Street

Here are a couple of shops that might appear on Strange Street. There's a farmacy. That's where chickens go to get medicine. There's also a pie cleaner. That's where you go to have your pies cleaned, of course! Think of ten other shops that belong on Strange Street. If you like, write a story about your shops, Strange Street, and the unusual things that happen there.

62

Hidden Treasure

Robert Louis Stevenson was born on November 13, 1850. He is the author of the classic adventure story *Treasure Island*. If you had a treasure, where would you hide it? Think carefully, because you wouldn't want to lose it, and you wouldn't want anyone else to find it either. Write down careful directions that will allow you to find your treasure even many years in the future. You can also draw a map.

Face Time

Stories often include great descriptions of people's faces. Here's a description of an imaginary character named Dibblyhoo, the World's Silliest Man: "He had big elephant ears, fuzzy caterpillar eyebrows, and google eyes." Here are three more characters: Dr. Goptar, the Wacky Genius; Princess Petunia; and Secret Agent Sam Steele. Describe the three characters' faces.

Happy Mouse Day

On November 18, 1928, the very first Mickey Mouse cartoon was shown. That makes November 18 Mickey Mouse's birthday. How do you think Mickey Mouse would celebrate his birthday? Write about it.

Group Exercise

"On a windy November day, Ted took a walk in the park." Copy this sentence down on a piece of paper. Then, you or someone in your class should add a second sentence. Pass it around until everyone in the class has added one sentence. As a group, you will have written a story!

Fan Mail

Think of someone to whom you would like to send a letter. It can be absolutely anyone—a famous athlete, a character on TV, someone from history. Make up an e-mail address for that person. For example, Abraham Lincoln might be HonestAbe@logcabins.com. Now, write an e-mail that you would like to send to that person.

(67)

Everything Day

Thanksgiving is known for turkey. The Fourth of July is known for fireworks. Christmas is known for presents. But what if there were one big holiday that mixed together all these holidays and more—with Halloween pumpkins and Easter eggs, too. Pretend this nutty new holiday is called Everything Day. Write a story describing your family during a typical Everything Day.

(68)

Rah, Rah, Shish-Bang-Boom

Here's a cheer:
    Hip hurrah hip hooray,
    We are going to win today.
    From the East to the West,
    You know we're the very best.
Make up your own cheer. It can be for yourself, your family, your school, your town, whatever. Just make sure you shout it loudly!

(69)

Turn That Smile Upside Down

Frown! November 19 is official "Have a Bad Day" Day! Make up an Extremely Awful Day Story that includes the following things: wet shoes, lost homework, a broken bicycle, and a messy food like spaghetti for lunch.

(70)

The First Thanksgiving

The fourth Thursday in November is Thanksgiving. This holiday is celebrated to honor a meal that the Pilgrims and Wampanoag Indians ate together way back in 1621. The Pilgrims were very thankful that the Indians were friendly and brought delicious foods like corn. Write a brief essay about something for which you are thankful.

Autumn Play

Here are two characters for an autumn play: Willard Wind and Kelly the Kite. Write some more lines for each character and finish the play.

Kelly the Kite: "I'm ready to come down, Willard. I've been up here a long time."
Willard Wind: "Should I hold my breath?"

Loopy Leftovers

Thanksgiving dinner is a very big meal. People often have lots of food left over. Come up with a list of ten ways to use your Thanksgiving leftovers. Be creative. Don't be shy about suggesting turkey pizza or cranberry and corn soup.

The Rules of the Game

The fourth week of November is National Game and Puzzle Week. Think of a game that you really like. It can be baseball or checkers or hide-and-seek. Write down the rules as carefully as you can so that other people can learn to play your favorite game.

Fly Like a Turkey

Benjamin Franklin wrote a letter to his daughter in 1784. In it, he said he wished the turkey had been chosen as the symbol of America instead of the eagle. Write your own Ben Franklin–style letter. Come up with some strong arguments for why the turkey should be America's official symbol.

Spiral Story

Writing in straight lines from left to right gets boring, don't you think? How about writing a spiral story. Start at the outer edge of a piece of paper and write around and around. This will help you get started: "The penny rolled through the crowded grocery store. Ricky Rounder chased after it . . ."

December

After December Comes . . .

December is the twelfth and final month of the year. But what if there were a thirteenth month? What would it be called? What new holidays would be celebrated during this month? For example, National Popsicle Day. Write a description of your made-up thirteenth month and let your imagination run wild.

Union Hill

On December 3, 1775, the very first official American flag was flown. What if you could design your own personal flag? Write about what colors and symbols you would choose and why.

Cookies

The first week of December is Cookie-Cutter Week. You've heard of the Gingerbread Man. Make up your own specially shaped cookie. It can be a gingerbread dinosaur or a chocolate chip cookie in the shape of a star. Will your cookie have sprinkles for eyelashes or will you draw a smiley face with frosting? Describe your cookie and draw a picture, too, if you like.

(79) Escape from Pickle Island

The bad news is that you are trapped on Pickle Island. The good news is that you have the following items: some rope, an empty bottle, a hula hoop, a balloon, a pencil but no paper, and a gum wrapper. What can you do with these items? Write a story in which you describe how you use them to either escape or call for help and get rescued.

(80) Brainiac

On December 8, 1894, Elzie Segar was born. He created the famous cartoon character Popeye. When Popeye ate spinach he instantly grew strong. Imagine a new character named Brainiac. When Brainiac eats asparagus he instantly grows incredibly smart. Write a story about the adventures of Brainiac.

(81) Walter Mitty Story

The writer James Thurber was also born on December 8, 1894. He created a famous character named Walter Mitty. Walter Mitty was just a regular guy. But in his imagination he did all kinds of heroic feats and had many exciting adventures. Are you like that, too? Think of an adventure you've had in your imagination. Put it down on paper as a story.

(82) Walking, Talking, Power Robot

Every December there's a brand new toy for sale that all the kids are excited about. Pretend you are the president of a toy company. Think up a new toy that everyone will want. Make sure it's something really cool, like a Walking, Talking, Power Robot. Now, write a TV advertisement that describes your new toy.

Hear, Hear

Car horns go "beep." A ball bouncing on the ground goes "bonk." Cats say "meow." Make up sounds for the following things: a rocking chair, a tomato splattering, a lightbulb burning out, water running in the sink, and a goldfish. Use your five made-up sounds in a story.

December Poem

December is a long word. But many words rhyme with it, including remember, September, timber, member, and even short words like fur and purr. Write a December poem using these and other rhyming words.

Four Words Hiding in Mississippi

Mississippi became the twentieth U.S. state on December 10, 1817. There are four words hidden in Mississippi: miss, sis, is, and sip. Write a short story using these words.

Classmate Interview

Newspaper stories are based on interviews. Pair up with classmates and ask one another interview questions. Remember to write down the answers your classmates give you. Then, write a story about your classmate based on the information you learn in the interview. Here are some interview questions to help you get started: Where were you born? Do you have any brothers or sisters? What is your favorite food? Do you play any sports?

The X-Force

Here are the four superheroes that make up the X-Force: Micro, a superhero who can become microscopically small; The Bolt, a superhero who can travel over wires and takes the form of human electricity; The Blur, the world's fastest superhero; Flexor, a superhero who can bend and stretch like a rubber band. Now, write an adventure starring the X-Force. You can even do it in comic book form complete with pictures.

88

Trivia

Are you good at trivia? Here's an easy one: Who was the first president of the United States? Answer: George Washington. Think up three pieces of trivia. Put your trivia questions on one side of an index card and the answers on the other. Quiz your classmates. You can even have a class-wide trivia tournament.

89

Town Monument

On December 15, 1832, Gustave Eiffel was born in France. He was an engineer who designed the Eiffel Tower in Paris and helped build the Statue of Liberty for New York City. What if you could create a monument for your town? Would it be a statue of a giant prairie dog, or maybe of a girl eating ice cream? Describe a town monument of your own design.

90

Zany Z Tale

The letter *Z* is a lot of fun. But it doesn't get used very often. How about shaking things up by using the letter *Z* instead of the letters *C* and *M*? A cat becomes a zat. A monkey becomes a zonkey. Write a Zany Z Tale and use the letter as often as you zan!

91

The Wright Stuff

On December 17, 1903, Orville and Wilbur Wright flew an airplane successfully for the first time ever. The Wright Brothers famous flight took place at Kitty Hawk, North Carolina. Can you think of other famous brothers or sisters? Write about what they accomplished.

Run-On-and-On Sentence

You can keep a story going just by adding "and then." Here's an example: "I woke up and then I brushed my teeth and then I ate breakfast and then . . ." Whew, seems like that could go on forever. Try writing your own "and then" story. Keep writing and then keep writing and then keep writing until you're all tired out.

Humbug Day

December 21 is Humbug Day in honor of the character Ebenezer Scrooge from Charles Dickens's book *A Christmas Carol*. If Scrooge didn't like something, he would shout out "Bah, humbug!" Write down five things you don't like. At the end of each dislike, write "Bah, humbug!" Here's an example: "Whenever I watch my favorite TV shows, commercials always come on. Bah, humbug!"

Mixed-Up Meals

A taco usually contains beef or chicken. A sandwich might have turkey or bologna. Pizza often has pepperoni or mushrooms. Make a list of ten mixed-up foods such as a mushroom taco or bologna pizza.

Being Paul Polar Bear

What do you think it's like to be a polar bear? What do you think goes on in a polar bear's mind? Are they happy, funny, hungry? Imagine that you are a polar bear. Then, write a story from a polar bear's point of view.

The Dinosaur Next Door

Dinosaurs became extinct millions of years ago. But what if dinosaurs were still around today? There would be dinosaurs in the woods along with bears and oak trees. Certain kinds of tame dinosaurs might live on farms along with cows and chickens. You could even have a dinosaur as a pet. Write a story about what it would be like now if dinosaurs still walked the earth.

Alpha-Train

Create an Alpha-Train and make it as long as possible. Here's how: Write a sentence in alphabetical order, such as "A big cow didn't enjoy funny games." That's a good train for letters *A* through *G*. It can be a silly sentence—as long as it's a sentence. See how far you can go.

Holiday Carol

You probably know some popular carols that are sung during the holidays. There's "Silent Night" and "Jingle Bells," for example. Write your own holiday carol. Make it very jolly and lots of fun.

Opposite World

What if snow was warm instead of cold? What if people ate hamburgers for breakfast and cornflakes for dinner? Think about a world where everything is the opposite. Now, write a story about Opposite World including as many upside-down . . . er, downside-up details . . . as you can imagine.

Scrapbook

December 31 is the very last day of the year. A lot has happened, hasn't it? Create a scrapbook for the year. Write about memorable events and include drawings and photos if you like.

January

Happy New Year!

January is the month when one year changes over to the next. But what if you had a time machine? Last year could be followed by a truly new and different year—1900, say, or 1776, or the year 3000. Would you use your time machine to travel into the past or into the future? Describe your adventure in a story.

New Year's Acrostic

Happy New Year! January 1 is the first day of a brand-new year. Create a "Happy New Year" acrostic. Choose words or phrases that relate to your wishes for the coming year. The *H*, for example, could be "Hope I'll make a new friend this year."

One Smart Cookie

Eating black-eyed peas is supposed to bring you good luck in the New Year. Make up special powers for other foods. Maybe cookies make you smart, or pickles make you laugh a lot. Create a menu of your food choices and their special powers.

Fly's-Eye View

What do you think things look like to a fly? A grain of salt looks very tiny to a person. Maybe a fly sees the same grain of salt differently. A fly might describe it as "a large white cube, about the same size as one of those big blocks of sand." Think of five different objects. Describe what each would look like from a fly's point of view.

Get Your Flashlight Hat!

People who run stores have to sell some pretty strange things. For example, if you ran a shoe store you might have to sell purple cowboy boots. One way to get people interested would be to create an advertisement. "We've got them! You need them! Be the first in your neighborhood to own a pair of stylish and comfortable purple cowboy boots!" Pretend you run a department store. You have to sell 500 hats with flashlights attached. Create an ad to help sell them.

Smithtown

January 6 is National Smith Day, in honor of all the people named Smith. It's the most common last name in the English language. There are two million Smiths in the United States. But what if everyone were named Smith? It would be really confusing, right? Jimmy Smith would ride his Smith bicycle down Smith Street to Smith's Grocery Store to pick up some Smith's Chicken Noodle Soup. Write a story about a town where everyone and everything is named Smith.

Scrambled Story

"School from Billy home came. Bear a house the was in." Unscramble these two sentences. Then finish this story.

The Write Stuff

January 8 through 14 is Universal Letter-Writing Week. Do you have a friend or relative who lives far away, even in another town or country? Write that person a letter and describe your plans for the new year.

The Next Big Thing

January is National High-Tech Month. Think about all the high-tech inventions that exist today: CD players and computers and video games and cellular phones. What kind of new invention do you think the world needs next? What would make life easier or help you to do things faster? Write about a high-tech gadget that you would like to invent.

Slogans

Many places have slogans. For example, America is sometimes called "The Land of the Free." Missouri is called "The Show-Me State." Chicago is called "The Windy City." Make up slogans for your house, your neighborhood, your town, your state, and for America.

Poetry Break

January 13 is Poetry Break Day. Take a break and write several verses to finish the following poem.

I look up at the sky and I see the moon
I go to the zoo and I see a baboon
I go to the store and I see . . .

Nutty and Nuttier

Comedian Jim Carrey was born on January 17, 1962. He's the star of such movies as *Ace Ventura: Pet Detective* and *Dumb and Dumber*. Pretend Jim Carrey is the star of your own movie and write the mini-script. Make sure it's weird, wild, and very funny.

Why Are You Always Feeding Me Fish?

January 22 is Answer Your Cat's Question Day. What a weird day! But what if a cat could ask you questions? What would it ask? Write down five cat-to-human questions—and your human-to-cat answers, too.

Get Vivid

Question: "What kind of dog is that?"
Answer: "It's just a dog."

Don't you hate it when someone gives you a really boring answer like that?

Try again and make your description exciting and fun.

Question: "What kind of dog is that?"
Answer: "It's a fun, friendly dog. It loves to run and play catch and roll in the grass. Its name is _____".

Silly Soup

January is National Soup Month. Pretend you are a chef and you have created a secret recipe for something called Silly Soup. Silly Soup has 25 different ingredients! They are the wackiest things you can think of—bubblegum and ice cubes and cat food and wristwatches. Write down your recipe for Silly Soup, and don't forget—a good batch requires 25 different ingredients!

Simile Jubilee

A simile is a phrase that compares two things using the words like or as. Here are some examples: "He ran like the wind." "It was easy as pie." Use at least five similes in a short story.

Winter on Trial

Imagine that the season of winter is on trial for being too cold, too long, and too boring. You are a lawyer and it is your job to defend winter, telling the jury the good things about winter, such as making snowballs and drinking hot chocolate.

This will help you get started: "Ladies and gentlemen of the jury. Before you today sits winter, accused of being cold, too long, and too boring. But I would like to argue that . . ." Now, complete this speech and convince the jury that winter is a good season.

Gold Rush Tale

On January 24, 1848, gold was discovered in California. That started a gold rush. People poured into California hoping to get rich. Finish the following gold rush tale:

_____ (man's name) had just arrived in California from _____ (which state?). He had a thick beard and _____ (describe his face), he was wearing _____ (describe clothes), and . . .

Sounds Like . . .

January 28 is National Kazoo Day. How would you describe the sound a kazoo makes? One example might be: "A kazoo sounds like a goose screaming at the top of its lungs." Come up with five imaginative descriptions for other musical instruments, too, such as pianos, guitars, and drums.

Oprah

Oprah Winfrey, the famous television talk show host, was born on January 29, 1954, in Kosciusko, Mississippi. Imagine that you are on Oprah's show. Write down the questions Oprah might ask you. And write down your answers, too.

Strange Udderance

Adding something strange to a normal situation can start a story. You and your family are at the table eating dinner. That's pretty normal, right? But when you pour yourself a glass of milk, the milk carton says "Mooooo." There's the start of a story. Finish it.

State of the Town

Late in January, the president of the United States often delivers an important speech called "The State of the Union." In this speech, the president talks about various things that might be important to Americans: new laws, disasters such as hurricanes, or exciting scientific discoveries. Write a "State of the Town" speech in which you discuss good things and bad things currently happening where you live.

Say What?

Dialogue is one of the most important parts of writing. It involves writing down what characters say to each other. Create a story by finishing this conversation between Katrina and Eleanor.

"I have a secret," says Katrina.
"Oh, please tell me. Please, please," begs Eleanor . . .

Food Combos

What if you combined a cranberry and a banana? You would have a cranana. Write about a mixed-up food combination of your own. What would it be called? What would it look like? Could it be used in a new juice or as an ice cream flavor?

Random Writing

Cut out a whole lot of words from a newspaper or magazine. Cut out single words, as many as 20 or 25. Put them in a hat or a box. Close your eyes, reach in, and select five words. Use those words to write a short story.

February

Freedom Writer

February 1 is National Freedom Day. In honor of this special day, take a moment to think about some symbols of freedom: the flag, the Liberty Bell, eagles. Do you have a favorite symbol of freedom? Do some research at the library or on the Internet. Then, write a mini-essay about why this symbol is important to you.

Favorite Saying

There are so many great sayings. "An apple a day keeps the doctor away." "A penny saved is a penny earned." What is your favorite saying? Write about what the saying means and why it is important to you.

Inkblot

Look at the inkblot below. If you look at it long enough maybe it won't look like an inkblot anymore. What does it look like to you? Write about what you see.

Winter Wear

It's winter now. Across much of the United States it is very chilly. Dream up some clothing items you would like to invent for winter. Try to come up with ten really out-there ideas, such as ski sneakers so you don't have to wear boots.

Really Chilly

The coldest day ever recorded anywhere in North America happened on February 3, 1947. In the tiny town of Snag, Canada, the temperature was minus 81 degrees Fahrenheit. Pretend you're a television weather forecaster in the town of Snag. Write down the weather report you would give on that incredible day. This will help you get started: "Good evening, ladies and gentlemen. Brrr. It's a chilly one . . ."

I Meant That as a Compliment

February 6 is official Pay-a-Compliment Day. Here's a compliment: "You are a very good writer. You really know how to tell a good story." Think of compliments for the following five people: a teacher, a parent, a friend, a neighbor, and someone you see every day, like a bus driver. Write them down.

Story Time

The time that a story takes place is very important. At the top of a piece of paper, draw the face of a clock, with the numbers one through twelve. Next, draw in the clock's hands so that it tells time. Now, write a story that takes place at the time you chose. If you picked midnight, it might make sense to write a scary story. If you chose 5:30 in the morning, you might want to write a story about a person who is fishing and watching the sunrise.

Little House in Tahiti

Laura Ingalls Wilder was born on February 7, 1867. She is famous for her series of *Little House* books about growing up on the prairie as a pioneer. Write your own pioneer story about growing up in an unusual place. It can be *Little House in the Rainforest* or *Little House in Tahiti*. Have fun and let your imagination roam.

Fortune Cookies

Have you ever had a fortune cookie? Inside the cookie, there's a piece of paper with a message. Sometimes the message is a prediction about your future. Sometimes it's a piece of good advice. Write down five messages that you would like to find inside fortune cookies.

A Tale of Two Tuttles

February 2 is the second day of the year's second month. Seems like a good day for a story about a pair of twins. This will get you started: "Mack and Zack Tuttle were known as the Tuttle Twins. The Tuttle Twins talked alike, dressed alike, and even rode everywhere on a tandem bicycle. One day, while they were both eating double-dip ice cream cones . . ."

Magic Words

A wizard has given you three magic words. Saying "Crazzabelam" makes you invisible. Saying "Frappa Wappa" makes any object you choose grow larger. Saying "Slobibble" makes any object you choose become very, very tiny. Write a story in which you use the three magic words.

Stardust Memories

The spacecraft *Stardust* was launched on February 7, 1999. It will travel three billion miles. It will be gone from the earth for five years. Its mission is to gather samples of comets. The *Stardust* is unmanned, meaning no people are on board. No one will get to see all the places it travels. Aren't you curious? Create a *Stardust* Flight Log and write down some of the exciting things you think will happen during the spaceship's long, long trip.

Pennies for Your Thoughts

Abraham Lincoln was born on February 12, 1809. Take a look at a penny; it has an image of Lincoln on the front. Now, trace around the penny to create a circle. In that circle, write a word that describes Lincoln. For example, you could write "tall." Using one piece of paper, see how many penny outlines you can fill with words about America's sixteenth president.

My Magazine

The first issue of the first magazine published in America appeared on February 13, 1741. It was called *American Magazine.* Its editor was Andrew Bradford. What if you could create your own magazine? What would you call it? Would it cover sports or movies or what? Write a story for your magazine.

The Sun Is Yellow, the Grass Is Green

Here's a well-known Valentine's Day poem:

> Roses are red.
> Violets are blue.
> Sugar is sweet.
> And so are you.

Make up your own Valentine's Day poem using different objects or other colors: red fire trucks, for example, or green grass.

Animated Objects

Imagine that something that cannot talk could suddenly speak. Your choice can be any object—a tree, a lightbulb, a car, an old pair of blue jeans. (Don't pick an animal. They already "speak" with purrs and barks and growls.) Now, think about what your object would say. Would it speak in a sweet or a gruff voice? What kind of personality do you imagine this object would have? Write a story in which you describe this amazing talking object.

Cucumber Phone

There are regular telephones and there are cell phones. But what if there were such a thing as a Cucumber Phone? Who would call you on a Cucumber Phone? What kind of things would he or she say? Ring, ring! Better get that, someone's calling you on the Cucumber Phone. Write about the caller and describe your conversation.

Dear Diary . . .

Samuel Pepys was born in England on February 23, 1633. He's a famous diarist. He's still remembered all these years later because he kept very detailed diaries. Come up with a diary entry for today. Make it exciting and full of details like Samuel Pepys' diary, so that people will still find it interesting in 400 years!

The Odd Triple

Here are three of the strangest friends ever: a firefighter who loves chocolate milk, a race car driver who always gets lost, and a rock star who also has a pet python. What names would you give each of these characters? Create an adventure story for these three unusual friends.

Fairy Tale

On February 24, 1786, Wilhelm Grimm was born. The Brothers Grimm, Wilhelm and Jakob, wrote some of the greatest fairy tales ever, such as *Cinderella* and *Snow White*. Make up a similar story of your own. Remember, it can be very strange and surprising—that's what makes it a fairy tale.

Cool New Sport

Think of a new winter sport. It can be something strange like playing golf on skis. Let your imagination glide and describe the rules of your made-up new sport.

The World's Biggest Sandwich

Have you ever read the *Guinness Book of World Records*? It has all kinds of strange records: the person with the longest fingernails, the loudest rock band ever. Write about a strange record that you would like someone to set.

Eel E-Mail

Eels are long, snake-like fish that live in the ocean. Imagine that there's one named Edgar Eel who actually can be reached by e-mail. His address is Edgar.Eel@DeepintheOcean.com. Write an e-mail to Edgar. Ask him about living in the ocean and tell him all about life on land.

Movie-Star Name Game

Do you know how to play the Movie-Star Name Game? Take your middle name and combine it with the town in which you were born. Say, for example, there is a girl named Melissa Amber Jones who was born in Denver. Her movie-star name would be Amber Denver. What's your movie-star name? Make up the plot of a movie in which your own personal star would appear.

Travelogue

Arizona's Grand Canyon became a National Park on February 26, 1919. Have you ever visited there? It's an amazing place. Think about a beautiful, natural place that you have visited. It can be a lake or a beach or a mountain range. Then, write down everything you can remember: how it looked, whether it was warm or cold, any animals that you saw. Make your description exciting and beautiful so other people who read it will also want to visit.

March

Magic Yellow Umbrella

March is National Umbrella Month. Use this prompt to start a story that celebrates this useful invention. "On Rudy's eighth birthday his parents gave him an umbrella. It was big and bright and yellow and magic. Yes, magic! When Rudy opened the umbrella . . . "

Pig Power

March 1 is National Pig Day. In honor of this wacky holiday, write a story about a heroic pig. Maybe the pig saves some skiers trapped in an avalanche. Or maybe this hero pig catches some criminals.

Some Assembly Required

What if you had the following: a hammer and nails, blue paint, some square pieces of wood, some panes of glass, six wheels, a kite, a flashlight, a bicycle horn, and a fan. What would you build? Dream up a cool invention. Then, write down instructions so that someone else can make one, too.

The Cow That Says "Wow!"

Theodor Geisel was born on March 2, 1904. He's better known as Dr. Seuss. One of his most famous books was *The Cat in the Hat*. Write a rhyming story featuring your own Dr. Seuss–style character. It can be "The Mouse in the House," or "The Cow That Says 'Wow!'"

Texas Independence Day

March 2 is Texas Independence Day. On this day in 1836 Texas gained its independence from Mexico. Do some research at the library or on the Internet and write down ten facts about this great state.

Backhanded Exercise

Have you ever heard somebody say: "I know that like the back of my hand"? How well do you know the back of your hand? Study it for a while. Then write a description. Be as detailed as you possibly can.

The Crumpets

Imagine there's a TV show called *The Crumpets*. It features four main characters. Mr. Crumpet is a policeman. Mrs. Crumpet is a karate expert. Their daughter Missy Crumpet is always getting into mischief. They have a dog named Waldo. Now, write a short episode of the imaginary TV show, *The Crumpets*.

Seymour Stars, Inventor of Powerful New Telescope

Alexander Graham Bell was born on March 3, 1847. He invented the telephone. Isn't it strange that the man who invented the telephone was named Bell? Dream up five inventions and fittingly named inventors to go along with them. For example, you could have a pocket fan invented by Wendy McBreeze.

Autograph Week

Autograph Collecting Week runs from March 5 to March 11. Who is someone that you would like to collect an autograph from? Write about why you like or respect this person.

Prefix Madness

A unicycle has one wheel. A bicycle has two wheels. A tricycle has three wheels. Make up some new words, using the prefixes "un" and "bi" and "tri" in front of some other words. For example, a "tripencil" could be a pencil with three points and three erasers. Make up ten new words, and make sure you also write down what they mean.

Singing a Different Neptune

Pretend that you are a visitor to Earth from the planet Neptune. When you return home you will want to describe Earthlings to your fellow Neptunians. But what if you don't have a word for "eyes" in the Neptunese language? You might have to describe them as "shiny balls that humans use to see." Now, describe what a person looks like to your friends on Neptune. But do not use the following words: eyes, mouth, teeth, tongue, lips, nose, ears, hair, arms, legs, hands, feet, fingers, or toes. Good luck! Or as Neptunians say, "Urk bliff!"

In-action, Un-adventurous Films

Each year on March 6, the Boring Institute gives out its Most Boring Film Awards. What is the most boring movie you've seen recently? First, rate the movie in terms of "Zs." Maybe it gets seven Zs: Zzzzzzz. Then, write a review. Describe why this particular movie was so awfully, incredibly, terribly boring.

State-Ments

What is Mom making for dinner? Answer: *Don't know, Alaska.* Get it? (I'll ask her.) Make up at least three of your own State-ments. Hint: Delaware, New Jersey, Washington, Missouri, Ohio, Utah, and Maine all work well.

Excuses, Excuses

March 6 through 12 is National Procrastination Week. *Procrastination* means putting off duties and making all kinds of excuses. Be creative and write down a really imaginative excuse for why you can't clean your room this week. This will help you get started: "I'm so sorry. I really want to clean my room. But, you see, the most incredible thing has happened . . ."

March Man

Pretend there's a new superhero known as March Man. He has special powers, such as his Super Flower-Power Ray. Design your own March Man trading card, with a picture and a description. Then, trade cards with your classmates.

P. I. Joe

On March 9, 1959, the very first Barbie dolls appeared in toy stores. What if you could create your own doll or action figure? (It can be male or female.) What would you name it? What would it be—a spy, a basketball player? Pretend you are creating an advertisement in a toy catalog and write a description of your doll or action figure.

Knock-Knock Jokes

Knock-Knock Jokes are a lot of fun! Here's an example:

Knock, Knock!
Who's There?
Lettuce.
Lettuce Who?
Lettuce In!

Make up your own Knock-Knock Joke and write it down.

The Buck Starts Here

The first paper money in the United States was issued on March 10, 1862. What if you could create your own bill? What would it be: a $1 zillion bill, maybe? Whose picture would you put on it? On a piece of paper, design your own bill. Look at real bills for ideas. Your bill should have various sayings and slogans written on it—"Official Money of the Town of Muskogee, Oklahoma," for example—just like a real bill.

Tongue Twister

Here's a tongue twister: "Fuzzy-Wuzzy was a bear. Fuzzy-Wuzzy had no hair. Fuzzy-Wuzzy wasn't fuzzy, was he?" Try saying that five times fast. Now, create your own tongue twister. Hint: Use lots of rhyming words and use the same letters over and over.

Wendy Watermelonseed

March 11 is Johnny Appleseed Day. Do you know about Johnny Appleseed? He walked all over the United States during the 1800s planting apple seeds. Some of the trees he planted are still alive today. Imagine there was a Peter Pumpkinseed or a Wendy Watermelonseed. Write a story about your character's adventures.

Relativity

Albert Einstein was born in Germany on March 14, 1879. When people think of a genius, they often think of this famous scientist. But who do you think of as a genius? Does a genius have to be someone who is smart at solving complicated math problems? Or can a genius be someone who is exceptionally good at other things—a genius at video games, for example, or a genius at making friends? Write about a person you think of as a genius and explain why.

Green Tale

St. Patrick's Day is March 17. This is a big day for the color green. Think about how many things are green: emeralds, frogs, grass, and lettuce. Write a story using at least five different green things.

Great Seal

March 18 is International Day of the Seal. Create a "Great Seal of the Seal." This can be similar to the great seal of your own home state. Draw a picture of a seal. Then, surround the picture with written slogans and facts about these fascinating animals.

Remember That Tune

March 21 is Memory Day. Think about how many different songs you have heard during your life. Try to remember as many song names as you possibly can. Make a list and make it long.

The Grass Is Always Bluer

Taxis are usually yellow. Stop signs are usually red. But what if taxis were pink? What if stop signs were purple? Write a story using all they mixed-up colored things you can think of.

April

Keep America Beautiful

April is Keep America Beautiful Month. Do you have some ideas on how to help do this? Picking up garbage from parks is one good idea. Giving houses a fresh coat of paint is another. Create a Keep America Beautiful poster that includes your ideas.

Class Clowns

Do you like a good joke? April happens to be National Humor Month. Here's a joke for you: *What did the flower say to the bee?* Answer: *Buzz off.* Think up some jokes of your own and write them down. Trade jokes with your classmates and laugh, laugh, laugh.

Signs

Signs are everywhere. Some restaurants have signs that say, "Please wait to be seated." Stores sometimes have signs that say, "No dogs allowed." Think of five signs that you think should exist. What would they say? Where would you put your five signs?

Shhhh!

April is Listening Awareness Month. Be real quiet and listen very carefully for five minutes. What do you hear? Chances are you will hear new things that you wouldn't notice if you weren't paying very careful attention. Describe every different sound you hear.

The Opposite Brothers

Oscar and Otis are the Opposite Brothers. When Oscar wears black, Otis wears white. When Oscar walks, Otis runs. Write a story about the Opposite Brothers.

April Fools!

"There's a new kind of gum called Forever-Chew. You can chew it for hours and hours and the flavor never goes away. It changes flavors, too. First, it's grape, then it's peppermint, then it's cinnamon. Would you like a stick? Really? April Fools!" Now, write your own tricky tale. Remember at the end to write, "April Fools!"

Ferret Care

Many people have dogs or cats or fish as pets. But some people have ferrets, which are a strange and unusual kind of pet. Do some research on ferrets at the library or on the Internet. Then, pretend you're going on a trip. Your friend has promised to take care of your pet ferret. But what does it eat? Does it stay in a cage sometimes? Can it go outside by itself like a cat or a dog? Write a note for your friend with instructions on how to take care of your pet ferret.

Express Mail

The very first Pony Express rider began his trip on April 3, 1860. He had a bag full of letters to deliver and he traveled from St. Joseph, Missouri, to Sacramento, California. It took ten days, but this was considered very fast mail service. Remember, this was more than 100 years before e-mail. Do some research on the Pony Express. Then, pretend you were alive during the days of the Wild West. Write an imaginary letter to be delivered by the Pony Express.

(184)

Space Exploration

Space is fascinating. It's full of distant stars and speeding comets and unexplored planets. April 3 through 9 is Astronomy Week. Write about what you think is out in space. Are there any tiny planets the size of marbles? How about time warps? Do you think there are other living creatures in space?

(185)

The Class Courier

Create your own class newspaper! Write a story about something interesting that happened recently. Maybe there was an exciting sports event. Or maybe your favorite band has a new CD. If you combine stories from everyone in class, you'll have a complete newspaper. It will have all kinds of stories on all kinds of subjects. You might even give your paper a name.

(186)

The Long Sleep

Washington Irving was born on April 3, 1783. He wrote a famous story called *Rip Van Winkle* about a man who went to sleep and woke up 20 years later! What do you think would happen if you slept for 20 years? How would the world have changed when you finally woke up?

Add "Van Winkle" to your last name. For example, if your name is Marcy Phillips, you become Marcy Van Winkle. Then, write a story about waking from a 20-year nap.

(187)

The 100-Meter Sack Hop

The first modern Olympics were held in Athens, Greece, on April 6, 1896. The Olympics is a huge event with competitions in many different sports: swimming, skiing, and running, for example. What's something you are really good at that you would like to add to the Olympics? Do you wish there was kickball at the Olympics, or hopscotch? It can even be something strange like holding your breath underwater. Write a sports story about your very own Olympic event.

The Skinny on Olive Oyl

Famous gossip columnist Walter Winchell was born on April 7, 1897. Pretend that you write a gossip column for the newspaper. Your job is to write gossip items about various cartoon characters. This will help you get started: "Snow White was spotted at a local beach, trying to get a suntan. Meanwhile, I have learned that Spider Man loves apples. Maybe we should be calling him Cider Man . . ."

In Bad Shape

Some things have their own special shapes, right? But what if donuts were square? What if wheels were triangular? Finish the following story and make sure you change lots of shapes: "Jill took a square CD out of its round box. She could not believe it! Her eyes grew large and rectangular . . ."

Oceans of Fun

April 9 through 15 is National Week of the Ocean. More than half the Earth is covered by oceans; they're full of whales and strange fish. Do some research at the library or on the Internet and write down ten fun facts about the ocean.

Paul Revere's Midnight Ride

On April 18, 1775, American patriot Paul Revere took his Midnight Ride. Use the library or Internet to do some research on this famous event. Then, write a short play about Paul Revere's ride.

Loads of Labels

Have you ever noticed how many words are on a food label? There is the food company's name, an advertising slogan, a description of the food, the ingredients, even a recipe sometimes. Create your own label. It can be for any kind of food—cereal, taco shells, sloppy joe mix—whatever makes you hungry. Give your product a fun name like "Big Bill's Baked Beans," and remember to include lots and lots of information on the label.

Iceland When It Sizzles

April 20 is officially the first day of summer in Iceland. It's a big national holiday! What do you think summer is like in Iceland? Do you think it ever gets very warm? Do you think people in Iceland eat ice cream in summer? Pretend that a girl named Bjork lives in Iceland and is your friend. Come up with five questions for an imaginary e-mail that you could send her.

Exact-o World

Welcome to Exact-o World. This is a place where words are exactly as they sound. A *butter knife* is a knife made out of butter. A *cowboy* is a young male cow. *Boxing gloves* are gloves that fight each other. Write a story that takes place in Exact-o World. Be very exact. And let your imagination run wild . . . but make sure it doesn't escape!

Write a Writer

What is your all-time favorite book? Who is the author? Write a letter to the author. Tell the author how much you enjoyed the book. Maybe ask some questions, too. How did the author dream up the idea for the book? Does the author have any tips on how you can become a great writer, too?

Raining Cats and Dogs

In many places across the United States, the month of April means lots of rain. Have you ever heard the saying, "It's raining cats and dogs"? That's a strange saying, right? What if it really did rain cats and dogs? Write a story about what would happen.

Spring Cleaning

Spring is a time when people like to clean their houses and get a fresh start. If you could clean up absolutely anything, what would it be—your room, your town, the world? Write a story about a giant spring cleaning job.

Kindergarten

Frederich Froebel was born on April 21, 1782. This famous German educator invented many children's toys and also invented kindergarten! What kinds of things do you think are important to learn in kindergarten? What do you wish you had learned at that age? Write a lesson plan with recommended activities for kindergartners.

Personal Power Words

What are some words that you like? They can be anything—*ripple, violet, fusebox*, you name it—as long as they're words you think are cool. Pick out five of them. These are your Personal Power Words. Write a short story using your chosen words.

April Really Bugs Me

There are insects known as mayflies and June bugs. Make up a bug with April in its name—an "Aprilflea" for example. Write a description of your imaginary insect.

May

Hatching a Story

May is National Egg Month. Finish this eggs-cellent tale. "The egg was light blue, the size of a football, and had red and yellow spots. It began to crack and out popped . . ."

Jumbo Burger

May is National Hamburger Month. Imagine that you have opened a new restaurant called Jumbo Burger. Make up a menu listing all the different things you would offer, and don't forget to give the prices. Maybe there would be a Triple Jumbo Burger with cheese—$1.75. Or a Wacky Meal with fries—$2.50. Create your own mouthwatering Jumbo Burger menu.

Nursery Rhyme Time

May 1 is Mother Goose Day. When you were younger, did you have a favorite nursery rhyme—Humpty-Dumpty, maybe, or Old Mother Hubbard? Maybe you have a younger brother or sister who enjoys nursery rhymes. Create a nursery rhyme and make it lots of fun for little kids.

Uniforms

When you write stories, it may be useful to know how to describe various uniforms. For example, firefighters wear boots and hats and long slickers. Look in a book or magazine and find an interesting person wearing a uniform. Describe that uniform as carefully as you can.

Imaginary Pen Friend

Pen Friends Week is May 1 through 7. Imagine that you have a pen friend in a faraway country—Russia or Egypt or Brazil. Do some research on that country at the library or on the Internet. Think of some questions you'd like to ask about that country, and put them in a letter to your imaginary pen friend. Remember to give your pen friend a name that matches with the country he or she is from.

Loyalty Day

May 1 is Loyalty Day by a special presidential proclamation. Do you think loyalty is important? Write a story about a loyal friend or a loyal pet.

Backpacking

How about playing a game called Backpacking? Think of a person's name and an item that starts with the same letter. Now, work your way through the alphabet, *A* to *Z*. This will get you started. "My name is Alice. I'm going backpacking and I'm taking an anteater."

Weather Report

May 4 is National Weather Observer's Day. How does the weather look? What is your prediction for tomorrow? What will the temperature be? Will it be windy? Will there be any rain? Write a weather report with your predictions for the next five days.

Wacky Critter

Some real-life animals have very strange names, such as *orangutans* and *koala bears*. Make up a weird and wacky animal of your own and describe what it looks like, where it lives, and what it eats.

(210) Spinning a Yarn

Imagine a character named Kelly Kitten. Write down ten different sentences about Kelly. Make sure that you write each sentence on a separate line. Now, cut out each of the ten sentences. Then, tape them together, one after the other. You will have a single, long, skinny story. It should look something like a piece of yarn that Kelly the Kitten might play with.

(211) Cinco de Mayo

In Mexico, May 5 is called *Cinco de Mayo*. It's a big national celebration, with music and dancing and food. Do some research at the library or on the Internet. Then, make a list of ten facts about Mexico.

(212) Short Month, Long List

May is the month with the shortest name—only three letters long. Many other words have only three letters such as *bat* and *hat* and *dot*. Make a long list with all the three-letter words you can think of. Write a story using at least ten of your words.

(213) Inventory

An *inventory* is a list of all the items in a particular place. For example, an inventory of a room might include "bed, dresser, mirror, shoes," and so on. Pick a place: your house, your classroom, a store. Then, create an inventory. Think hard and try to list everything that you can think of.

214

"Scooter Wins By a Claw . . ."

Each year on May 5, a lobster race is held in the town of Aiken, South Carolina. Sounds pretty strange, doesn't it? Write a sports story about an exciting race between five lobsters named Scooter, Shelly, Bubbles, Red, and Clawdius.

215

Greetings from Fiji

National Postcard Week starts on May 7. Pretend you are visiting the coolest place you can imagine: the Fiji Islands, or China, maybe. Do some research on this very cool country. Then, write a postcard to a friend from this place. If you like, you can also draw a picture on the front of the postcard.

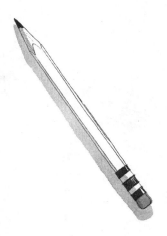

216

Lisa's Lemonade

May 10 is National Small Business Day. If you could start a small business, what would it be: a lemonade stand, maybe, or a lawn mowing service? Give your business a snappy name and create an advertisement. Remember, you want your ad to be exciting and full of information so that people will want to use your business.

217

Idiom's Delight

"I aced that test." The English language is full of these kinds of colorful phrases. They're called *idioms*. You don't take them literally. *Acing a test* doesn't mean turning a test into a playing card, right? It means scoring really high—high like an ace. Now, fill in the blank and create five of your own idioms. "I _____ that test." For example, "I sewered that test" could mean you did really, really poorly.

Tacofest

May 12 and 13 is Picklefest in Atkins, Arkansas. There's a pickle-eating contest and a pickle beauty contest and all kinds of other silly events. Think up your own silly festival. It can be anything: Mushroomfest, Tacofest, or Sausagefest. List ten events that you would have at your festival.

Colorful Story

Stories are always better when they mention lots of bright colors. Write a story and fill it with as many colors as you can: plump red tomatoes, yellow taxi cabs, and green, green grass.

"We're Not in Kentucky Anymore"

L. Frank Baum was born on May 15, 1856. He wrote *The Wonderful Wizard of Oz*. In this story, there are famous characters such as the Tin Man, who needs a heart, and the Lion, who needs courage. Here are three new characters: Cheetah wants to run fast. The Stone Statue wishes he could laugh. Dottie wishes to return home to Kentucky. First, read *The Wonderful Wizard of Oz*. Then, write an Oz-style story and describe how these new characters' dreams come true.

Secretabub Codegop

Here's a secret code. On all words that end with a consonant, place "abub" at the end of the word. On all words that end with a vowel, place "gop" at the end of the word. Now, write a message in secret code and exchange it with a classmate. Goodabub luckabub crackingabub thegop codegop!

Abigail Supersleuth

Arthur Conan Doyle was born on May 22, 1859. He wrote many famous stories about a made-up detective named Sherlock Holmes. Write your own detective story using a character named either Arnold or Abigail Supersleuth. This will help you get started: "The mansion's bedroom window was open. The diamonds and rubies and other jewels were missing . . ."

All-Four-One

Mia Hamm is a famous soccer player. Marie Curie is a famous scientist. Sally Fields is a famous actress. Sally Ride is a famous astronaut. Roll all four of them into one and you have Mia Marie Fields Ride, the world's first soccer-playing, scientist, astronaut actress. Write a story about this wacky woman.

Birthday Song

How come the only song people hear on their birthday is "Happy Birthday"? Shouldn't there be another birthday song called "It's Your Big Day" or "Cake and Candles"? Think of some great new words and write a brand-new birthday song.

Wild, Wild West

Wild Bill Hickok was born on May 27, 1837. He's a famous figure from the Wild West. Here are some new mean and ornery Western-style characters: Tough Terry McGillicutty, One-Eyed Pete, Bronco Betty, and her horse Thunder. Put these characters into a Western story.

June

Volunteers

June 1 through 7 is International Volunteers Week. If you could volunteer to help out around your town, what would you do? Would you clean up trash, maybe, or deliver meals to people who are sick and cannot leave their homes? Think about what you would like to do as a volunteer. Write about your choice of volunteer activity and why being a volunteer is important.

Garage Sale

On June 3 each year, the world's largest garage sale is held in South Bend, Indiana. Usually about 12,000 people attend! What if you had a garage sale? Make a list of ten things you own that you would like to sell.

Worth a Thousand Words

There's a famous saying: "A picture is worth a thousand words." Find a photograph that you like. It can be in a book or a magazine or a newspaper. Study it closely. Then, write about what you think is happening in the photograph.

Pet Appreciation

The second week of June is Pet Appreciation Week. Do you have a pet? If not, what kind of animal would you like to have as a pet—a cat, a parrot, maybe a goldfish? Write as complete a description of your real or imaginary pet as you can, mentioning the kind of animal your pet is, what it eats, what it looks like, its personality, and so on.

230

Picnic

Every year on June 10 there's a "Betty Picnic" held in Grants Pass, Oregon. Everyone in the whole world named Betty is welcome. What if there were a picnic held for everyone with your name? Who are some famous people with the same name as you? Write a story about this unusual picnic.

231

Cool Creations

Summer is here and the weather is getting hotter. You know what that means. Ice cream! Now, what if you could invent your own special ice cream flavor? Would it be something like chocolate peanut-butter banana swirl? Pretend you own an ice cream shop. Create a menu listing at least ten new delicious flavors of ice cream of your own invention.

232

June Juggling Month

June 20 is World Juggling Day. Imagine if you tried to juggle a skunk, a can of purple paint, and a cowboy hat. Write a story about the mixed-up results.

233

Space Address

Your space-alien friend Iplik wants to send you a postcard. But first you need to give him your full address. Fill in the blanks:

_____ (name),
_____ (street address),
_____ (city), _____ (country),
_____ (planet), _____ (galaxy).

Make your address as detailed as possible to make sure Iplik's postcard reaches you.

Hall of Fame

There's a Baseball Hall of Fame, a Football Hall of Fame, even a Rock-and-Roll Hall of Fame. What kind of Hall of Fame would you like to see: fashion models, maybe, or all-star wrestlers? Make a list of members of your own special Hall of Fame, and also write down some reasons why each member was chosen.

A Fat, Yellow Hippo Smartly Dove Into Four Warm Ponds

"The quick brown fox boldly jumped over a tall fence." Rewrite this ten-word sentence ten times. Each time you rewrite it change just one word. For example, sentence number-one might read: "The quick brown cow boldly jumped over a tall fence." Sentence number-two might read: "The quick brown cow gracefully jumped over a tall fence." By the time you are finished you should have a very different sentence.

For Your Own Amusement

What if you had your own amusement park? You could give it a great name, like Wade's Wild World. What types of rides would you have? You could have some really fun ones, like a Triple Upside-Down Scream Coaster. Write about an amusement park you would build. Remember, give it a great name and fill it with all kinds of exciting rides.

April May March

It has been a long school year. Many different months have passed. Write a few sentences using the names of different months in various ways. For example, "April" could be a girl's name. Bands and soldiers "March." You "May" be able to write some interesting sentences.

238

Dr. Doolittle Vacation

When the famous fictional character Dr. Doolittle wanted to go on vacation, he would close his eyes and place his finger on a map. Wherever his finger pointed, that's where he would travel. Plan a Dr. Doolittle Vacation. Close your eyes and touch your finger to a map or globe. Do some research and write about the place you chose.

239

Pretend Postcard

Pretend you are a visitor to your own town. Does your town have some interesting places or special types of food or sports teams? Write a postcard describing an imaginary visit to your own home town.

240

Stretch Your Senses

It's pretty easy to describe how roses smell. It's pretty easy to describe how spaghetti and meatballs taste. But how about stretching your senses? Describe roses and spaghetti using a different sense than the one you would usually depend on. What does it feel like to touch a rose? How do spaghetti and meatballs look? If you enjoy this, try some other sense-stretching exercises, such as: What does salt sound like?

241

Bat Nights

The hottest days of summer are known as the "dog days." Can't you almost picture a dog panting in the heat? Well, how about making up your own descriptive names for other parts of the year? Maybe the days in early April are "flower days." Or maybe the nights close to Halloween are "bat nights." Think of ten and let your imagination go "hog wild"—or is it "kangaroo wild"?

242

Elvis Is Everywhere

Elvis Presley is famous for rock songs such as "Hound Dog" and "Burning Love." He was so popular that he was known as "The King." He died in 1977. Or did he? Some people think he got tired of all his fame and decided to go into hiding. Every now and then someone will claim to have seen Elvis still alive and walking around. Imagine that you spotted Elvis. Where would he be? At the mall, maybe, or working as a teacher? Would he be wearing a disguise? Write a story about spotting Elvis the King.

243

Summer Fashion Review

Every summer there are new styles of clothes: new types of shorts and sneakers, new swimsuits, or popular new T-shirts. Have you noticed any new fashions for this summer? Write a review discussing one or more of them. Remember reviewers have to be tough. They must express strong opinions, such as: "Sneakers with blue stripes are popular this summer. I think they look terrible, because . . ."

244

Sheer Nonsense

Some of the very best stories are full of nonsense. Humpty-Dumpty was an egg who fell off a wall. Who ever heard of that? Here's a bit of nonsense to get you started on a story of your own: "Watookie had on her favorite pink overalls. She was singing 'Happy Birthday' to no one in particular, and was gathering sticks for a stick pie. She ran into Mr. Chompers, the blue mule. Mr. Chompers was headed off to Soap Bubble City . . ."

245

Summer Job

When you are older you may have a job during the summer. Maybe you will be a lifeguard, or perhaps you will work in a music store. Write about your perfect summer job.

Fractured Fairy Tale

Write your own silly version of a well-known fairy tale. Instead of the Three Little Pigs you could write about the Three Big Cows. Instead of having Cinderella ride inside a pumpkin carriage you could have her fly onboard a zucchini plane. Have fun and let your imagination go bonkers!

Summertime and the Writing Is Easy

The school year is about to end. You are about to enjoy a nice, long summer vacation. So just relax. Let yourself write freely. Get loose, go wild, and put down whatever thoughts come into your mind. Write fast and free and have lots of fun!

Sentence Starters

Here are some sentence starters: A, No, I, The, and People. Write five sentences. Start each sentence with one of these words. For example, "I can't believe that summer is about to start!" That's a sentence that starts with I. Now, write five sentences using the five sentence starters.

Cool Colors

Colors have some pretty cool names like hot pink and sky blue. Think up ten new color names, like sun yellow or asparagus green.

Summer Fun List

What are ten fun things you want to do this summer? Make a list so you won't forget. And have a great summer!